BRAIN GAMES®

WHEEL OF FORTUNE

WORD PUZZLES

pil

Publications International, Ltd.

Let's get social!

⊙ @Publications_International

🛈 @PublicationsInternational

🛈 @BrainGames.TM

www.pilbooks.com

PUZZLES

Brain Games® Wheel of Fortune Word Puzzles is for everyone who wants to test their puzzle solving skills, as if they were a contestant on the show. No need to pay $250 for a vowel or land on Lose A Turn as you decode more than 150 puzzles. Solve puzzles from a wide range of categories that you see featured on the TV show. Each puzzle will show you which letters are remaining but remember a letter can be used more than once when you're filling out the spaces. In this book there are no skipped turns and you're the only competitor. Keep guessing until all the puzzles are revealed!

AROUND THE HOUSE

Solve the puzzle using 10 remaining letters. HINT: A super sticky solution.

D _ _ _ _ E - _ _ D E D
D _ _ _   _ _ E

Answer on page 158.

PHRASE

Solve the puzzle using 8 remaining letters. HINT: Look alert!

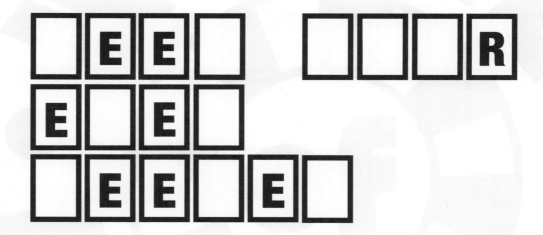

Answer on page 158.

BEFORE & AFTER

Solve the puzzle using 13 remaining letters. HINT: Really inspiring representative?

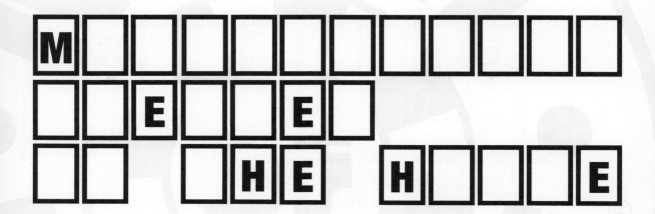

Answer on page 158.

SHOW BIZ

Solve the puzzle using 5 remaining letters. HINT: Short, but sweet.

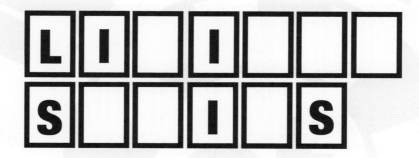

Answer on page 158.

BEST SELLER

Solve the puzzle using 4 remaining letters. HINT: Can you keep it?

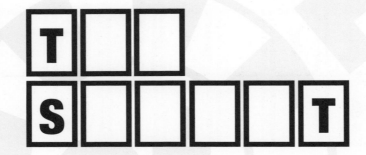

Answer on page 158.

THINGS

Solve the puzzle using 7 remaining letters. HINT: Feed them, and they could feed you.

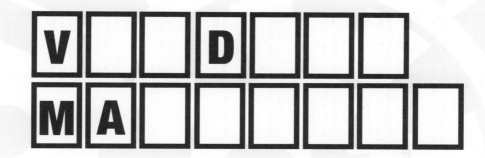

Answer on page 158.

CHARACTER

Solve the puzzle using 6 remaining letters. HINT: He's fully charged.

Answer on page 158.

WHAT ARE YOU DOING?

Solve the puzzle using 6 remaining letters. HINT: Use your noggin.

Answer on page 158.

CLASSIC TV

Solve the puzzle using 6 remaining letters. HINT: Miami nice.

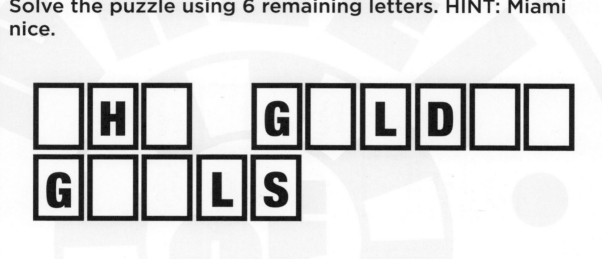

Answer on page 158.

PROPER NAME

Solve the puzzle using 5 remaining letters. HINT: His middle name is Bean.

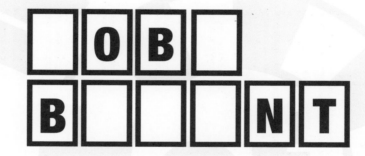

Answer on page 158.

EVENT

Solve the puzzle using 8 remaining letters. HINT: To the fire before the hire.

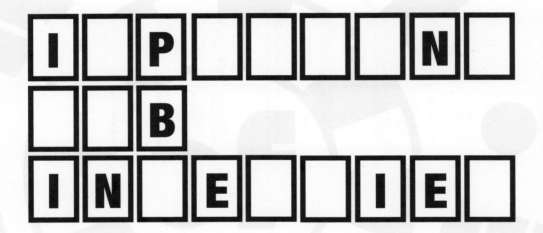

Answer on page 158.

RHYME TIME

Solve the puzzle using 5 remaining letters. HINT: Don't sleep on this one.

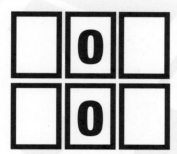 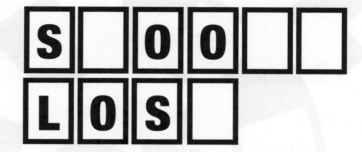

FAMILY

Solve the puzzle using 8 remaining letters. HINT: Aussie action actors.

Answer on page 158.

THING

Solve the puzzle using 8 remaining letters. HINT: A gift for the computer type.

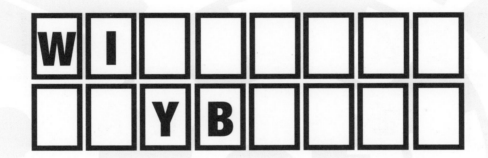

Answer on page 158.

FOOD & DRINK

Solve the puzzle using 8 remaining letters. HINT: A treat trifecta.

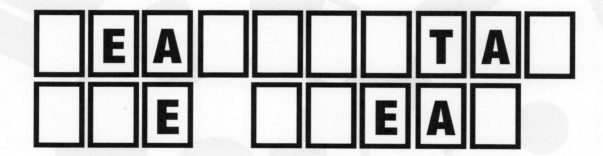

Answer on page 158.

SONG TITLE

Solve the puzzle using 8 remaining letters. HINT: A big hit for a great Brit.

FUN & GAMES

Solve the puzzle using 7 remaining letters. HINT: Got any threes?

Answer on page 158.

PLACE

Solve the puzzle using 6 remaining letters. HINT: Fun in the sun.

Answer on page 158.

IN THE KITCHEN

Solve the puzzle using 10 remaining letters. HINT: When you want just enough java.

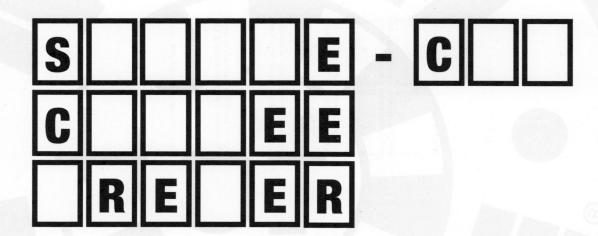

S _ _ _ _ E - C _ _
C _ _ _ E E
_ R E _ E R

Answer on page 158.

WHAT ARE YOU WEARING?

Solve the puzzle using 3 remaining letters. HINT: The night time is the right time.

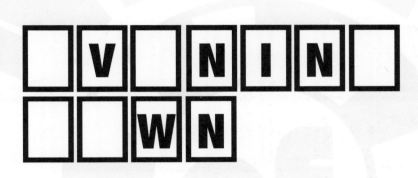

Answer on page 158.

LANDMARK

Solve the puzzle using 9 remaining letters. HINT: A "Windy" skyscraper?

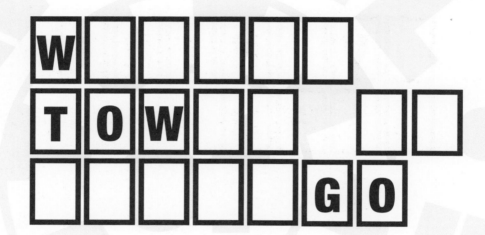

Answer on page 158.

LIVING THING

Solve the puzzle using 7 remaining letters. HINT: Some people find it fetching.

Answer on page 158.

THE 80'S

Solve the puzzle using 8 remaining letters. HINT: We never looked at music the same way again.

AROUND THE HOUSE

Solve the puzzle using 5 remaining letters. HINT: It takes batteries.

Answer on page 158.

MOVIE QUOTE

Solve the puzzle using 6 remaining letters. HINT: Fear is not an illusion.

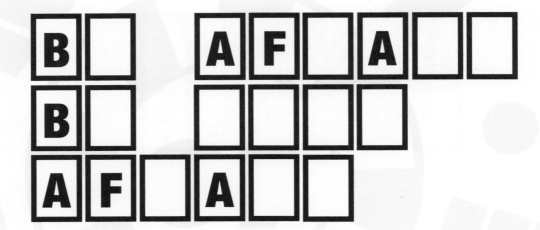

Answer on page 158.

PERSON

Solve the puzzle using 7 remaining letters. HINT: The answer is a parent.

Answer on page 158.

ON THE MAP

Solve the puzzle using 9 remaining letters. HINT: A great place to see stars.

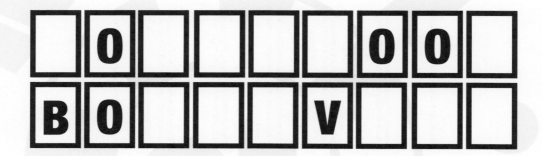

Answer on page 158.

THINGS

Solve the puzzle using 5 remaining letters. HINT: Some people write their own.

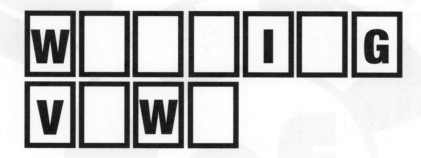

W _ _ _ I _ G

V _ W _

Answer on page 158.

OCCUPATION

Solve the puzzle using 5 remaining letters. HINT: They can give you a Lyft.

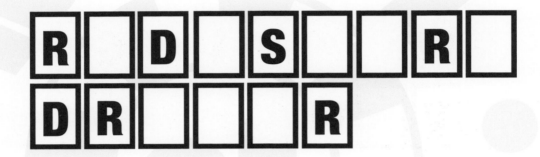

R _ D _ S _ _ R _

D R _ _ _ R

Answer on page 158.

FOOD & DRINK

Solve the puzzle using 6 remaining letters. HINT: Bread alert!

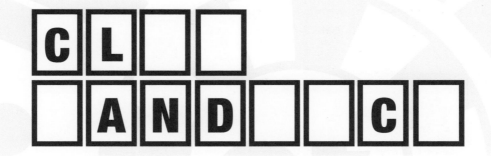

MOVIE TITLE

Solve the puzzle using 8 remaining letters. HINT: This one just sped by.

Answer on page 158.

WHAT ARE YOU DOING?

Solve the puzzle using 6 remaining letters. HINT: Cover to cover.

Answer on page 158.

PEOPLE

Solve the puzzle using 8 remaining letters. HINT: They like to play the field.

Answer on page 158.

EVENT

Solve the puzzle using 6 remaining letters. HINT: Everybody hide!

Answer on page 158.

PHRASE

Solve the puzzle using 9 remaining letters. HINT: A call for all to hear.

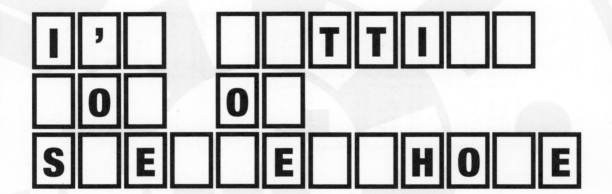

I'_ _ _ T T I _ _
_ O _ _ O _
S E _ _ E _ _ H O _ E

Answer on page 158.

AROUND THE HOUSE

Solve the puzzle using 8 remaining letters. HINT: They open up when other people are around.

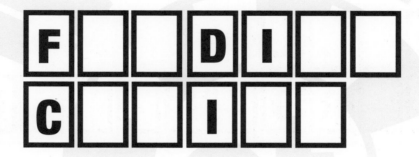

F _ _ D I _ _

C _ _ I _ _

PLACE

Solve the puzzle using 7 remaining letters. HINT: A little place to get a pint?

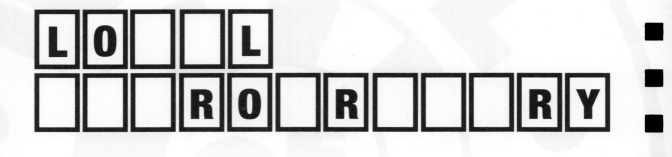

L O _ _ L
_ _ _ R O _ R _ _ _ R Y

Answer on page 158.

LIVING THING

Solve the puzzle using 6 remaining letters. HINT: Its heart can go 1,200 beats per minute.

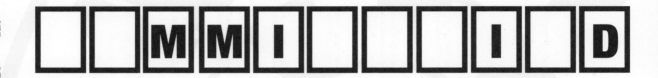

Answer on page 158.

PROPER NAME

Solve the puzzle using 7 remaining letters. HINT: A masterpiece master.

Answer on page 158.

BEFORE & AFTER

Solve the puzzle using 7 remaining letters. HINT: Locked in? Order in!

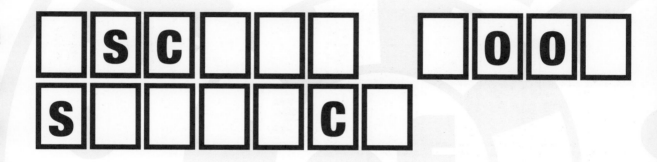

SONG TITLE

Solve the puzzle using 10 remaining letters. HINT: Some help to cross your problems.

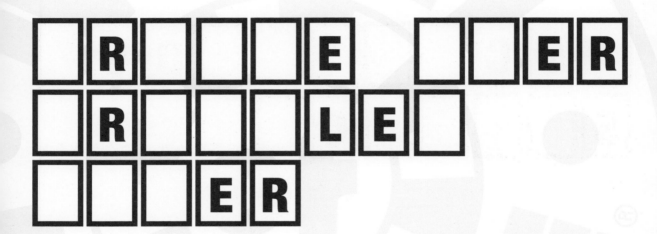

Answer on page 158.

CHARACTER

Solve the puzzle using 5 remaining letters. HINT: In real life, a helmet used by him sold for $898,000+.

Answer on page 158.

RHYME TIME

Solve the puzzle using 7 remaining letters. HINT: Don't miss out!

B _   _ _ _ R _   _ R
B _   _ Q _ _ R _

THING

Solve the puzzle using 6 remaining letters. HINT: It takes two.

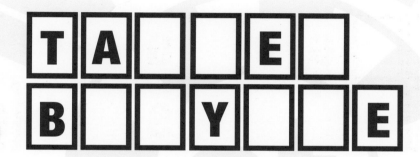

SAME LETTER

Solve the puzzle using 4 remaining letters. HINT: Topsy-turvy tunes.

S I _ G I _ G _ _ G

S I _ _ _ _ S _ _ G S

Answer on page 158.

WHAT ARE YOU WEARING?

Solve the puzzle using 9 remaining letters. HINT: A gem of an accessory.

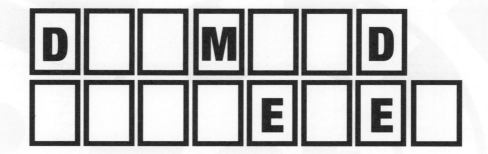

D _ _ M _ _ D
_ _ _ _ E E _

SAME NAME

Solve the puzzle using 6 remaining letters. HINT: The price is right on key.

D R ☐ ☐ & ☐ A R ☐ A ☐
☐ A R ☐ Y

Answer on page 158.

FUN & GAMES

Solve the puzzle using 4 remaining letters. HINT: It's filled with aluminum powder.

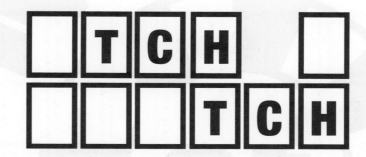

Answer on page 158.

SHOW BIZ

Solve the puzzle using 8 remaining letters. HINT:
Director's directions.

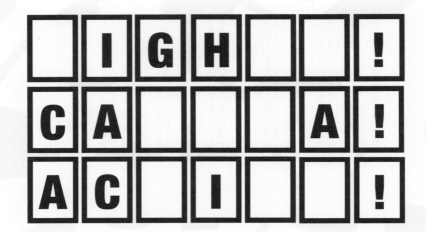

Answer on page 158.

ON THE MAP

Solve the puzzle using 10 remaining letters. HINT: A Keystone State cornerstone.

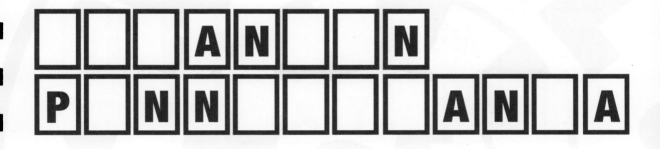

			A	N			N

P		N	N					A	N		A

WHAT ARE YOU DOING?

Solve the puzzle using 10 remaining letters. HINT: Tidying the turf.

Answer on page 158.

OCCUPATION

Solve the puzzle using 6 remaining letters. HINT: They're in charge of aisles and files.

Answer on page 159.

SONG/ARTIST

Solve the puzzle using 9 remaining letters. HINT: An explosive pop hit.

Answer on page 159.

PLACE

Solve the puzzle using 7 remaining letters. HINT: What's the answer? We're not telling.

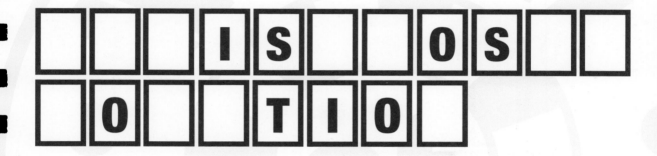

Answer on page 159.

QUOTATION

Solve the puzzle using 6 remaining letters. HINT: Is that all that bird can say?

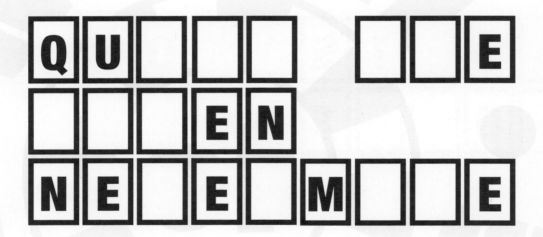

Answer on page 159.

AROUND THE HOUSE

Solve the puzzle using 5 remaining letters. HINT: You're getting warmer...

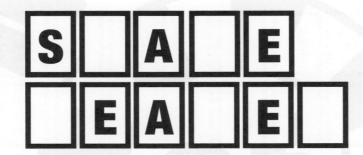

Answer on page 159.

STAR & ROLE

Solve the puzzle using 8 remaining letters. HINT: A knockout performance.

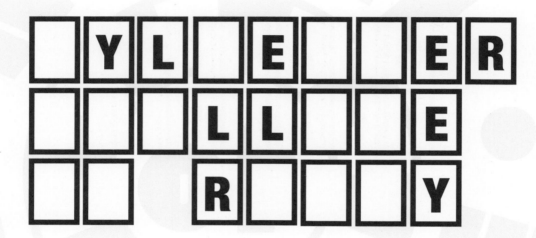

Answer on page 159.

THING

Solve the puzzle using 6 remaining letters. HINT: It gets to the point.

Answer on page 159.

THE 70'S

Solve the puzzle using 5 remaining letters. HINT: Let's put on our boogie shoes.

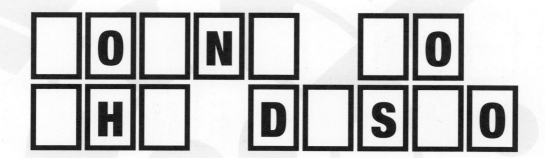

Answer on page 159.

FOOD & DRINK

Solve the puzzle using 6 remaining letters. HINT: Julia Roberts sang its praises in "Eat Pray Love."

WHAT ARE YOU WEARING?

Solve the puzzle using 8 remaining letters. HINT: They're quite the spectacles.

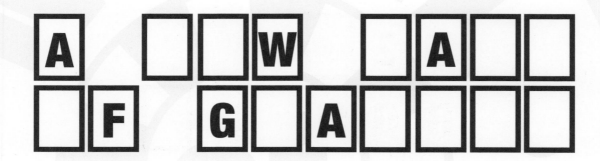

Answer on page 159.

FUN & GAMES

Solve the puzzle using 6 remaining letters. HINT: Mario? Super!

Answer on page 159.

THING

Solve the puzzle using 4 remaining letters. HINT: It can be juicy.

Answer on page 159.

ON THE MAP

Solve the puzzle using 9 remaining letters. HINT: This place was named for a king.

Answer on page 159.

LIVING THING

Solve the puzzle using 6 remaining letters. HINT: Senior spider?

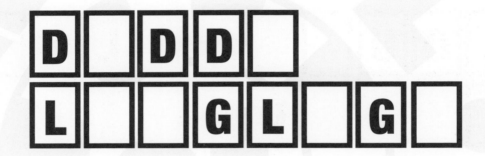

D _ D D _

L _ _ G L _ G _

Answer on page 159.

EVENT

Solve the puzzle using 6 remaining letters. HINT: It happens about twice a year.

Answer on page 159.

TITLE/AUTHOR

Solve the puzzle using 8 remaining letters. HINT: A story of constant refusal.

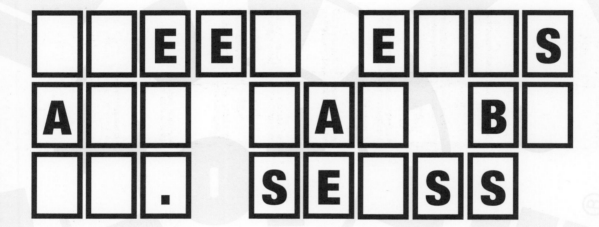

Answer on page 159.

WHAT ARE YOU DOING?

Solve the puzzle using 8 remaining letters. HINT: It works up a sweat.

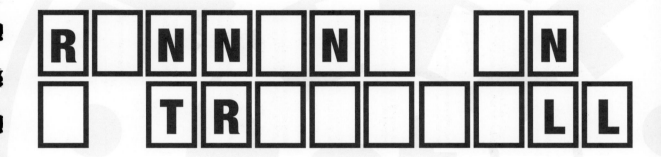

Answer on page 159.

TV TITLE

Solve the puzzle using 5 remaining letters. HINT: Supernatural streaming.

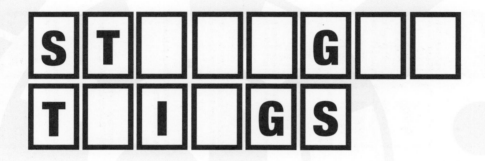

Answer on page 159.

BEFORE & AFTER

Solve the puzzle using 7 remaining letters. HINT: What Aladdin asked the genie for?

| | A | G | | C | | C | A | | | | |

| C | L | | A | | | |

Answer on page 159.

SONG LYRICS

Solve the puzzle using 6 remaining letters. HINT: As happy as a solar flare.

I'_ _ _LKI_ _
O_ SU_SHI_ _

Answer on page 159.

PHRASE

Solve the puzzle using 4 remaining letters. HINT: Eye cannot tell a lie.

| | | | I | N | | | I | |
| | B | L | I | | | I | N | |

Answer on page 159.

AROUND THE HOUSE

Solve the puzzle using 5 remaining letters. HINT: Oh, baby!

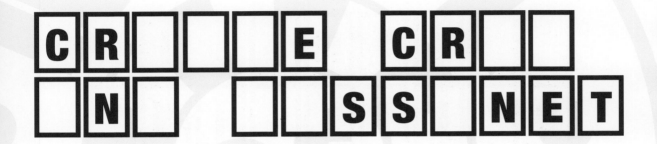

| C | R | | | E | | C | R | | |
| | N | | | | S | S | | N | E | T |

Answer on page 159.

PERSON

Solve the puzzle using 5 remaining letters. HINT: I hear you.

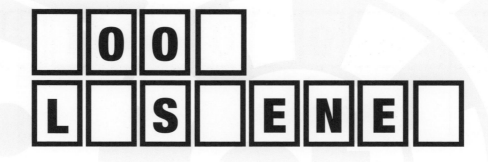

TITLE

Solve the puzzle using 6 remaining letters. HINT: A "worldly" publication?

⬜ O S M O ⬜ O ⬜ ⬜ T ⬜ ⬜

Answer on page 159.

PLACE

Solve the puzzle using 6 remaining letters. HINT: In the lap of luxury.

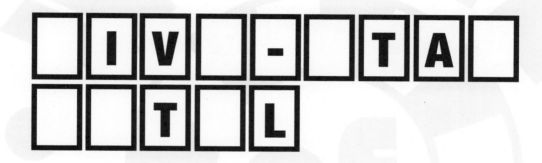

THE 90'S

Solve the puzzle using 8 remaining letters. HINT: Way cool with cool ranch?

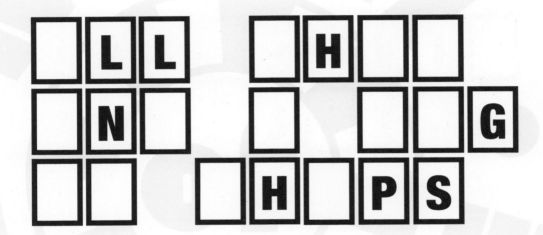

Answer on page 159.

THING

Solve the puzzle using 5 remaining letters. HINT: Say ahh...if you can.

TV QUOTE

Solve the puzzle using 3 remaining letters. HINT: A Stone Age shout.

Answer on page 159.

OCCUPATION

Solve the puzzle using 4 remaining letters. HINT: One who gets paid to make budget cuts?

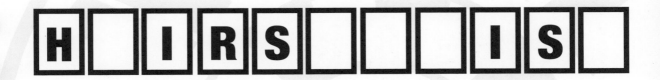

| H | | I | R | S | | | | I | S | |

Answer on page 159.

BEST SELLER

Solve the puzzle using 7 remaining letters. HINT: Billions of years in 250 pages.

Answer on page 159.

ON THE MAP

Solve the puzzle using 6 remaining letters. HINT: Charlize Theron and Dave Matthews were born there.

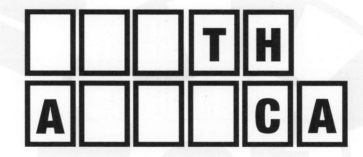

Answer on page 159.

CHARACTERS

Solve the puzzle using 11 remaining letters. HINT: Singing squirrels.

A _ _ _ N   A N _   _ H _
C H _ _ _ _ N _ _

Answer on page 159.

WHAT ARE YOU DOING?

Solve the puzzle using 4 remaining letters. HINT: CCing is believing.

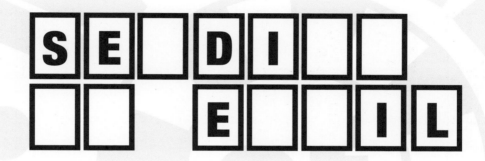

Answer on page 159.

IN THE KITCHEN

Solve the puzzle using 5 remaining letters. HINT: The big dipper.

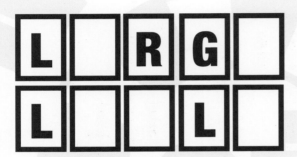 

L □ R G □   □ O U □

L □ □ L □

Answer on page 159.

PROPER NAME

Solve the puzzle using 6 remaining letters. HINT: Her work has people talking.

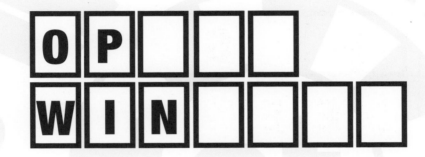

Answer on page 159.

EVENT

Solve the puzzle using 5 remaining letters. HINT: It can start the evening of Friday the 13th.

Answer on page 159.

WHAT ARE YOU WEARING?

Solve the puzzle using 5 remaining letters. HINT: A one-piece.

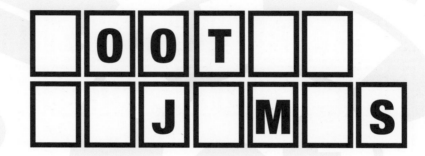

| | O | O | T | | |
| | | J | | M | S |

Answer on page 159.

CLASSIC TV

Solve the puzzle using 8 remaining letters. HINT: It was always sweater weather there.

M _ _ _ ER RO _ ER _ '
_ E _ _ _ _ OR _ OO _

Answer on page 159.

FOOD & DRINK

Solve the puzzle using 6 remaining letters. HINT: Found in the dairy section.

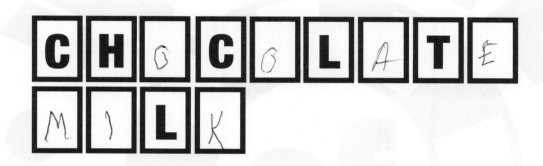

C H O C O L A T E
M I L K

LANDMARK

Solve the puzzle using 5 remaining letters. HINT: It just makes cents.

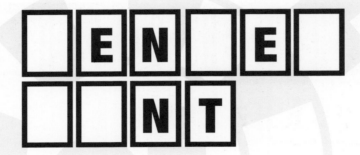

Answer on page 159.

SAME NAME

Solve the puzzle using 6 remaining letters. HINT: What has 4 wheels and a plug?

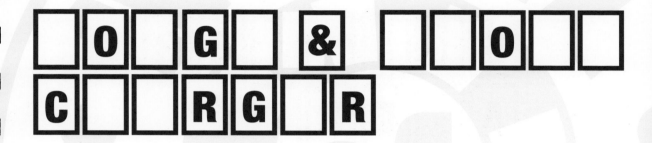

Answer on page 159.

PHRASE

Solve the puzzle using 5 remaining letters. HINT: Don't tell me how it ends!

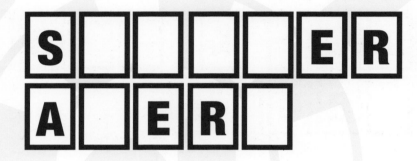

Answer on page 159.

AROUND THE HOUSE

Solve the puzzle using 3 remaining letters. HINT: Put a sock in it!

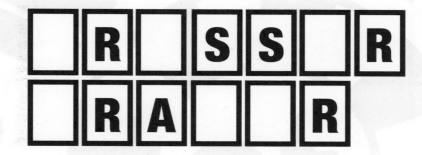

Answer on page 159.

BEFORE & AFTER

Solve the puzzle using 6 remaining letters. HINT: Sonny and Cher and a Yankees legend.

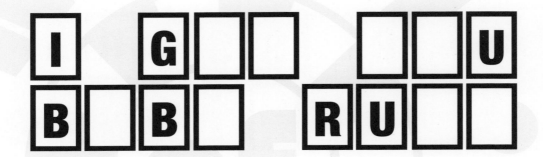

Answer on page 159.

LIVING THINGS

Solve the puzzle using 7 remaining letters. HINT: True fact: They've been known to laugh when they play.

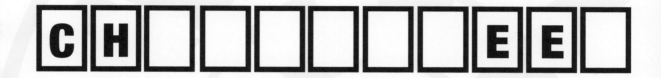

C H _ _ _ _ _ _ E E _

Answer on page 159.

WHAT ARE YOU DOING?

Solve the puzzle using 8 remaining letters. HINT: A meal so good, you want to enjoy it again.

E _ T _ N _

_ E _ T _ V E _ _

Answer on page 159.

MOVIE TITLE

Solve the puzzle using 7 remaining letters. HINT: Its soundtrack sold 1 million copies in a single week.

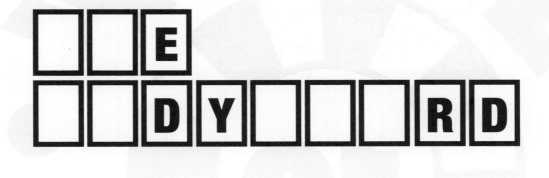

Answer on page 159.

THING

Solve the puzzle using 5 remaining letters. HINT: It follows your every move.

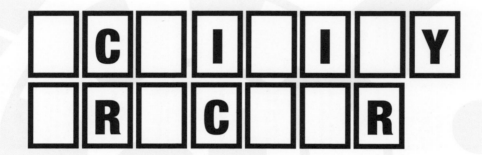

Answer on page 159.

FUN & GAMES

Solve the puzzle using 5 remaining letters. HINT: It's a team effort.

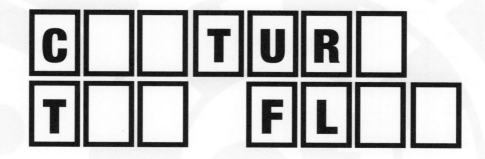

Answer on page 159.

SAME LETTER

Solve the puzzle using 6 remaining letters. HINT: A whole lot of nothing.

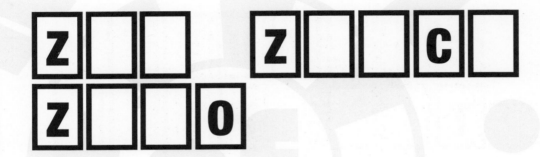

Z _ _ _   Z _ _ C _

Z _ _ O

Answer on page 159.

SHOW BIZ

Solve the puzzle using 6 remaining letters. HINT: Jane Lynch hosted one.

E _ _ Y _ _ _ R D S

_ E R E _ _ _ Y

Answer on page 159.

PLACE

Solve the puzzle using 5 remaining letters. HINT: Some dogs go here to learn how to act.

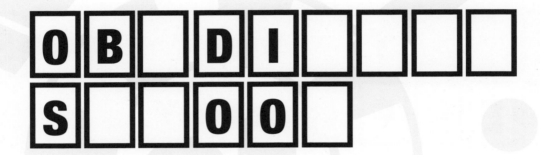

O B _ D I _ _ _ _
S _ _ O O _

Answer on page 159.

SONG TITLE

Solve the puzzle using 4 remaining letters. HINT: You might say this to someone moving your couch.

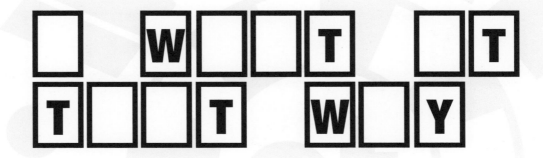

Answer on page 159.

AROUND THE HOUSE

Solve the puzzle using 6 remaining letters. HINT: Junior needs to do some cleaning up.

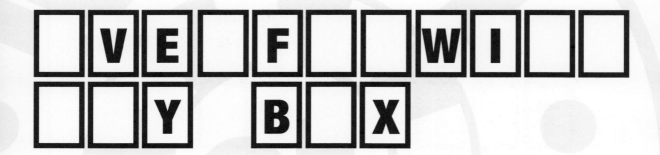

```
[ ][V][E][ ][F][ ][ ][W][I][ ][ ]
[ ][ ][Y][ ][B][ ][X]
```

Answer on page 160.

THING

Solve the puzzle using 7 remaining letters. HINT: A celebrity could endorse one.

Answer on page 160.

EVENT

Solve the puzzle using 6 remaining letters. HINT: A competition that's always abuzz.

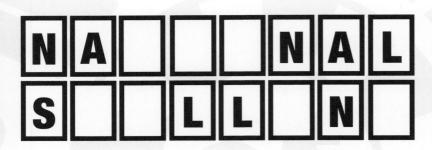

N A _ _ _ N A L
S _ _ L L _ N _   B _ _

Answer on page 160.

ON THE MAP

Solve the puzzle using 6 remaining letters. HINT: Peaks and valleys.

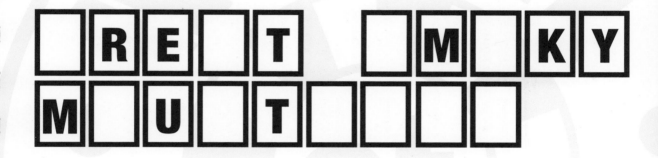

Answer on page 160.

FAMILY

Solve the puzzle using 5 remaining letters. HINT: Many fans are a "Sucker" for this sibling trio.

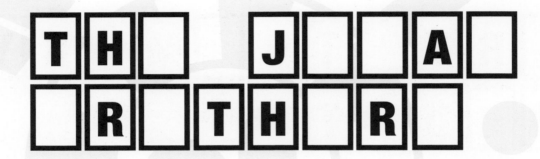

Answer on page 160.

WHAT ARE YOU WEARING?

Solve the puzzle using 5 remaining letters. HINT: This one's a little bit on the nose.

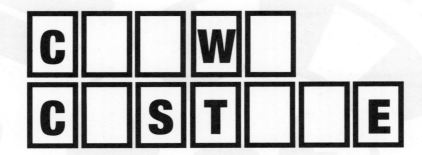

Answer on page 160.

FOOD & DRINK

Solve the puzzle using 5 remaining letters. HINT: It's all Greek to me.

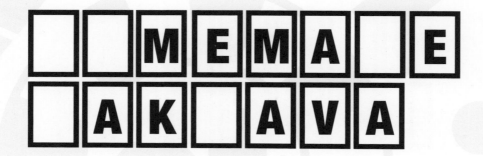

Answer on page 160.

PHRASE

Solve the puzzle using 5 remaining letters. HINT: This answer carries a little wait.

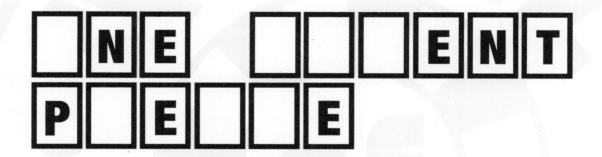

BEFORE & AFTER

Solve the puzzle using 8 remaining letters. HINT: "Superstition" superhero.

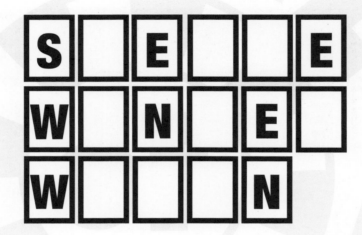

Answer on page 160.

TV TITLE

Solve the puzzle using 8 remaining letters. HINT: Jim Carrey auditioned to join the cast several times.

Answer on page 160.

PEOPLE

Solve the puzzle using 5 remaining letters. HINT: They have to make split decisions.

Answer on page 160.

SAME NAME

Solve the puzzle using 4 remaining letters. HINT: Both of them could use some sunlight.

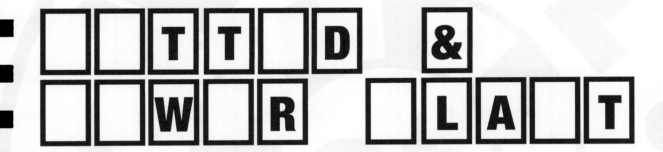

```
[ ][ ][T][T][ ][D]    [&]
[ ][ ][W][R][ ]    [ ][L][A][ ][T]
```

THING

Solve the puzzle using 8 remaining letters. HINT: Do a good job and you can get a round of this for free.

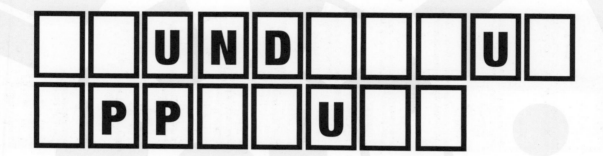

Answer on page 160.

AROUND THE HOUSE

Solve the puzzle using 5 remaining letters. HINT: One way to make an entrance.

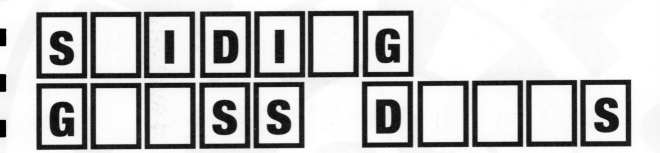

S _ I D I _ G
G _ _ S S _ D _ _ _ S

PHRASE

Solve the puzzle using 6 remaining letters. HINT: Join the popular thing!

JUMP ON THE
BANDWAGON

Answer on page 160.

SONG/ARTIST

Solve the puzzle using 8 remaining letters. HINT: A spelling lesson with soul.

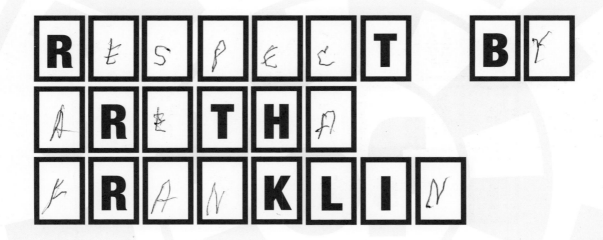

R E S P E C T   B Y
A R E T H A
F R A N K L I N

WHAT ARE YOU DOING?

Solve the puzzle using 8 remaining letters. HINT: Try to turn a couple bucks into millions.

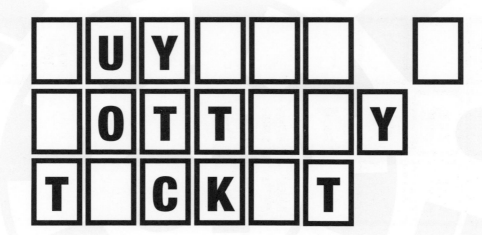

	U	Y				
	O	T	T		Y	
T		C	K		T	

Answer on page 160.

THINGS

Solve the puzzle using 5 remaining letters. HINT: They're known for traveling slowly.

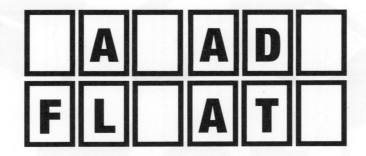

Answer on page 160.

PROPER NAME

Solve the puzzle using 4 remaining letters. HINT: He's got a lot of novel ideas.

S _ E P _ E _
_ I _ G

Answer on page 160.

WHAT ARE YOU WEARING?

Solve the puzzle using 4 remaining letters. HINT: Not a frozen asset, but an asset when things are frozen.

W _ N _ _ R
_ O A _

Answer on page 160.

OCCUPATION

Solve the puzzle using 5 remaining letters. HINT: A bill collector.

S U P E R M A R K E T
C A S H I E R

Answer on page 160.

BEFORE & AFTER

Solve the puzzle using 5 remaining letters. HINT: A warning heard at a family reunion?

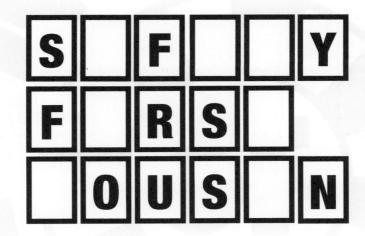

S		F			Y
F		R	S		
	O	U	S		N

Answer on page 160.

LIVING THINGS

Solve the puzzle using 8 remaining letters. HINT: They're spotted in Africa.

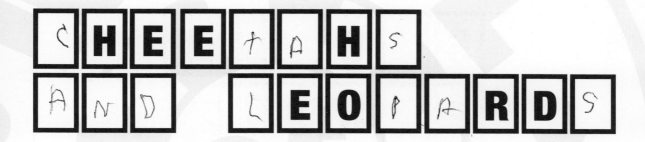

CHEETAHS
AND LEOPARDS

Answer on page 160.

FOOD & DRINK

Solve the puzzle using 6 remaining letters. HINT: It can get tossed around.

ROMAINE
LETTUCE

CHARACTERS

Solve the puzzle using 3 remaining letters. HINT: Their contracts might mention a Claus.

Answer on page 160.

PERSON

Solve the puzzle using 5 remaining letters. HINT: They'd like a nice bouquet.

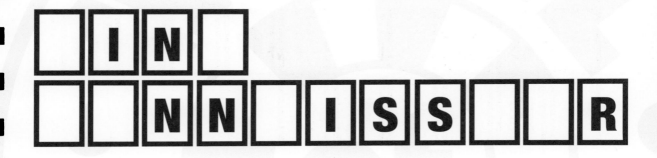

FUN & GAMES

Solve the puzzle using 5 remaining letters. HINT: Like Walk the Dog and Around the World.

Answer on page 160.

ON THE MAP

Solve the puzzle using 4 remaining letters. HINT: Population: 20 million plus.

S H _ _ _ H I _ _

_ H I _ _

Answer on page 160.

MOVIE TITLE

Solve the puzzle using 7 remaining letters. HINT: Tom Cruise's return to the air.

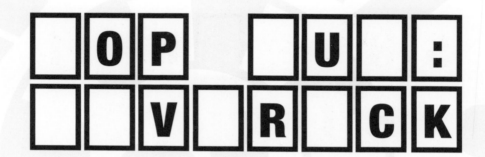

Answer on page 160.

EVENT

Solve the puzzle using 6 remaining letters. HINT: It's going, going to raise money.

Answer on page 160.

137

SAME NAME

Solve the puzzle using 7 remaining letters. HINT: Catch a snooze in a food-safe container?

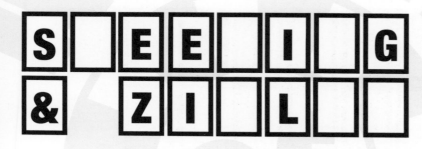

S _ EE _ I _ G
& _ ZI _ L _ _ _ _ _ G

Answer on page 160.

PHRASE

Solve the puzzle using 4 remaining letters. HINT: A bad day at the ballpark.

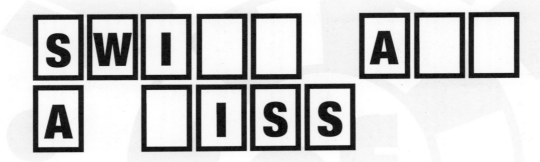

S W I _ _   A _ _
A _ _ I S S

Answer on page 160.

SHOW BIZ

Solve the puzzle using 8 remaining letters. HINT: Don't forget your lines!

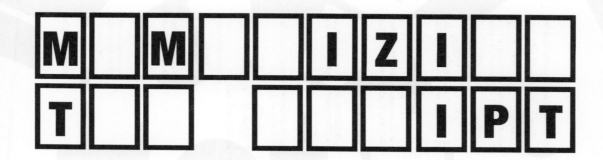

Answer on page 160.

PLACE

Solve the puzzle using 6 remaining letters. HINT: This spot's fantastic for paper or plastic.

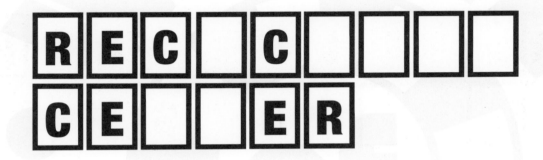

Answer on page 160.

WHAT ARE YOU WEARING?

Solve the puzzle using 7 remaining letters. HINT:
Dilapidated denims?

Answer on page 160.

MOVIE QUOTE

Solve the puzzle using 9 remaining letters. HINT: Take it step by step.

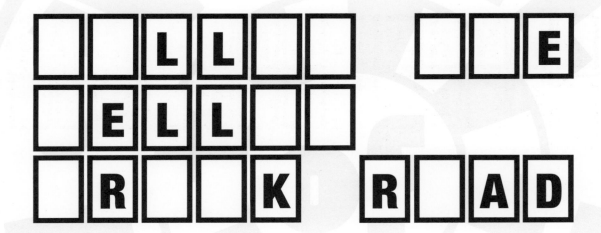

THINGS

Solve the puzzle using 6 remaining letters. HINT: They're totally digital.

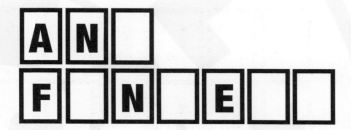

__NKY AN_

_N_EX F_N_E__

Answer on page 160.

OCCUPATION

Solve the puzzle using 4 remaining letters. HINT: They can put you in your place.

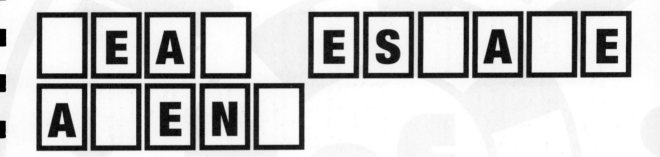

Answer on page 160.

CHARACTERS

Solve the puzzle using 7 remaining letters. HINT: A boy and his tiger.

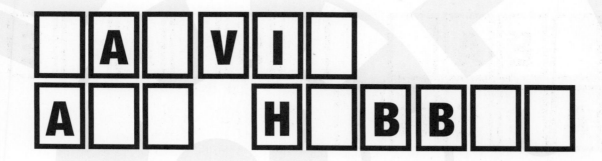

Answer on page 160.

AROUND THE HOUSE

Solve the puzzle using 6 remaining letters. HINT: What lies beneath.

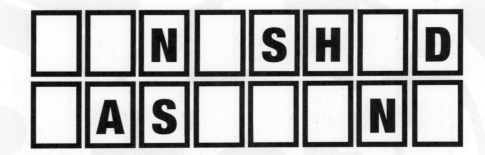

Row 1: _ _ N _ S H _ D

Row 2: _ A S _ _ _ N _

Answer on page 160.

SONG/ARTIST

Solve the puzzle using 9 remaining letters. HINT: A 6-minute epic sung by Freddie.

Answer on page 160.

FUN & GAMES

Solve the puzzle using 5 remaining letters. HINT: Careful with your big tow!

| | A | T | | R | | | I | | I | | G |

SAME LETTER

Solve the puzzle using 9 remaining letters. HINT: Precisely monitoring food intake.

C | R | E | | L | L |
C | | | T | | |
C | L | | R | E | S |

Answer on page 160.

PROPER NAME

Solve the puzzle using 5 remaining letters. HINT: Not the first First Lady.

E E _ _ _ R
R _ _ _ E V E _ T

TV TITLE

Solve the puzzle using 6 remaining letters. HINT: Who's making music in that costume?

```
[ ][ ][E]   [MA][ ][ ][ED]
[ ][ ][N][ ][ER]
```

Answer on page 160.

IN THE KITCHEN

Solve the puzzle using 5 remaining letters. HINT: It's another term for a high-stress situation.

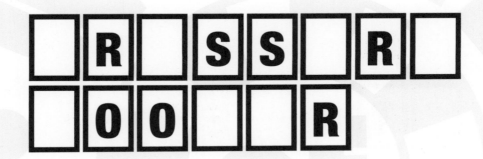

Answer on page 160.

PEOPLE

Solve the puzzle using 4 remaining letters. HINT: They're so unprofessional.

Answer on page 160.

LANDMARK

Solve the puzzle using 7 remaining letters. HINT: A place for loyal royal fans.

B U C _ I _ _ _ _
_ _ L _ C E

Answer on page 160.

BEFORE & AFTER

Solve the puzzle using 7 remaining letters. HINT: Oath to country and to keeping furniture shiny.

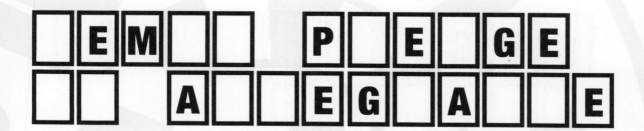

Answer on page 160.

THINGS

Solve the puzzle using 6 remaining letters. HINT: If you build it, they will come.

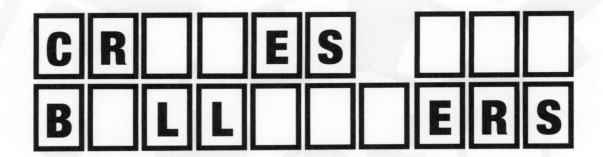

C R ☐ ☐ E S   ☐ ☐ ☐

B ☐ L L ☐ ☐ ☐ E R S

157

Answer on page 160.

ANSWER KEY

ANSWER KEY

PAGE 55
STORE MANAGER

PAGE 56
FIREWORK BY KATY
PERRY

PAGE 57
UNDISCLOSED
LOCATION

PAGE 58
QUOTH THE RAVEN
NEVERMORE

PAGE 59
SPACE HEATER

PAGE 60
SYLVESTER STALLONE
AS ROCKY

PAGE 61
PENCIL SHARPENER

PAGE 62
GOING TO THE DISCO

PAGE 63
PIZZA MARGHERITA

PAGE 64
A NEW PAIR OF
GLASSES

PAGE 65
NINTENDO SWITCH

PAGE 66
OFFICE GOSSIP

PAGE 67
LOUISVILLE KENTUCKY

PAGE 68
DADDY LONGLEGS

PAGE 69
LUNAR ECLIPSE

PAGE 70
GREEN EGGS AND HAM
BY DR. SEUSS

PAGE 71
RUNNING ON A
TREADMILL

PAGE 72
STRANGER THINGS

PAGE 73
MAGIC CARPET
CLEANER

PAGE 74
I'M WALKING ON
SUNSHINE

PAGE 75
SEEING IS BELIEVING

PAGE 76
CRADLE CRIB AND
BASSINET

PAGE 77
GOOD LISTENER

PAGE 78
COSMOPOLITAN

PAGE 79
FIVE-STAR HOTEL

PAGE 80
ALL THAT AND A BAG
OF CHIPS

PAGE 81
TONGUE DEPRESSOR

PAGE 82
YABBA DABBA DOO!

PAGE 83
HAIRSTYLIST

PAGE 84
A BRIEF HISTORY OF
TIME

PAGE 85
SOUTH AFRICA

PAGE 86
ALVIN AND THE
CHIPMUNKS

PAGE 87
SENDING AN EMAIL

PAGE 88
LARGE SOUP LADLE

PAGE 89
OPRAH WINFREY

PAGE 90
LONG WEEKEND

PAGE 91
FOOTIE PAJAMAS

PAGE 92
MISTER ROGERS'
NEIGHBORHOOD

PAGE 93
CHOCOLATE MILK

PAGE 94
DENVER MINT

PAGE 95
DODGE & PHONE
CHARGER

PAGE 96
SPOILER ALERT

PAGE 97
DRESSER DRAWER

PAGE 98
I GOT YOU BABE RUTH

PAGE 99
CHIMPANZEES

PAGE 100
EATING LEFTOVERS

PAGE 101
THE BODYGUARD

PAGE 102
ACTIVITY TRACKER

PAGE 103
CAPTURE THE FLAG

PAGE 104
ZIP ZILCH ZERO

PAGE 105
EMMY AWARDS
CEREMONY

PAGE 106
OBEDIENCE SCHOOL

PAGE 107
I WANT IT THAT WAY

ANSWER KEY